INSIDE COLLEGE FOOTBALL™

FOOTBALL IN THE BIG EAST CONFERENCE

ADAM B. HOFSTETTER

rosen publishing's
rosen
central®

New York

For Fazool

Published in 2008 by The Rosen Publishing Group, Inc.
29 East 21st Street, New York, NY 10010

Library of Congress Cataloging-in-Publication Data

Hofstetter, Adam B.
Football in the Big East Conference / Adam B. Hofstetter. — 1st ed.
    p. cm. — (Inside college football)
ISBN-13: 978-1-4042-1923-6 (hardcover)
ISBN-10: 1-4042-1923-4 (hardcover)
1. Big East Conference. 2. Football—East (U.S.) 3. College sports—East (U.S.) I. Title.
GV958.5.B34H64 2008
796.332'63—dc22

2007015224

Manufactured in the United States of America

On the cover: (*Top*): The Rutgers Scarlet Knights charge onto the field before a game against the Louisville Cardinals in November 2006. (*Bottom*): West Virginia Mountaineer running back Owen Schmitt (35) runs against the Louisville Cardinals' defense in a November 2006 game.

CONTENTS

INTRODUCTION

For most of its history, the Big East has been known more for basketball than for football. Only eight of the conference's sixteen full-time member schools even participate in football. But Big East teams have featured more than their share of football superstars. Players such as Jim Brown, Johnny Unitas, Dan Marino, Mike Ditka, and Larry Csonka lead the list of twelve NFL Hall of Famers who suited up for Big East schools before reaching the pros. Those players have been led by some of the best coaches ever to grace the game of football, from old-timers Glenn "Pop" Warner, Johnny Majors, Dick MacPherson, and Sid Gillman, to current standouts like Rich Rodriguez and Greg Schiano. Conference teams have played in memorable games and have been inspired by some of the most entertaining mascots in sports.

Louisville celebrates its Orange Bowl victory over Wake Forest on January 2, 2007.

However, things have not always gone well for the Big East. In fact, the conference almost folded in 2003. But thanks to some wise decisions by the conference leadership and the recent success of a few of its teams, Big East football is as popular today as it has ever been.

History of the Big East

The Big East conference didn't officially start playing football until 1991, but one team in the conference had been playing organized football since the earliest days of the sport.

A New Sport for the Country and for the Conference

On November 6, 1869, a team from Rutgers University (which was then called Rutgers College) won the very first college football game in history when it beat a team from the school now known as Princeton University by a score of 6–4. A few years later, officials from Rutgers and Princeton met in New York with representatives from Yale and Columbia Universities to establish the first set of formal rules for college sports—particularly the new sport of football. So, one of the oldest college football teams in history—Rutgers—now plays in one of college football's youngest conferences.

This artist's rendering shows what the first college football game—a Rutgers victory over the College of New Jersey (now Princeton) in 1869—might have looked like.

The Big East actually was founded in 1979, but at that time, it was focused mainly on basketball and did not compete in football at all. In fact, football powerhouse Penn State tried to join the Big East in 1982, but it got rejected because the conference wanted to keep the focus on basketball. That all changed in 1990, when Michael Tranghese became the conference's commissioner. Tranghese, who had been working for the conference since it was founded, made some big changes. The biggest one was his announcement, on February 5, 1991, that the conference would begin competing in Division I-A football.

Big East commissioner Mike Tranghese addresses the media in July 2004. At the time, Tranghese was struggling to keep the conference alive after football powers Miami and Virginia had left to join the ACC.

Are You Ready for Some Football?

To boost the conference's profile in college football, the Big East became a charter member of every major bowl agreement, including the current Bowl Championship Series (BCS). Tranghese even served as the head of the BCS for two years. But what really made the college football world take notice was when the Big East admitted four-time national football champion University of Miami, along with four other schools, into the conference just in time for the 1991 football season.

The Big East started the 1991 season with eight football schools: Boston College, Syracuse University, the University of

ACC commissioner John Swofford *(right)* shakes hands with Jim Weaver, Virginia Tech's athletic director, after the announcement of his school's departure from the Big East to join the ACC in July 2003.

Pittsburgh, and new members Miami, Rutgers University, Temple University, West Virginia University, and Virginia Polytechnic Institute and State University. Miami gave the Big East instant credibility as a major football conference and won the national championship in its first year in the Big East. Despite this quick start, the conference was experiencing some growing pains.

Trouble Brewing

Only half of the Big East's sixteen member schools actually competed in football, which was a very unusual setup in college sports.

In addition, the Big East's top basketball programs didn't like sharing the spotlight (or the conference's resources) with football teams. Tensions grew within the conference and led to constant rumors that the conference was unstable.

The Atlantic Coast Conference (ACC), whose territory overlapped with that of the Big East, took advantage of this rumored instability and apparent discontent. In 2003, the ACC announced that it was planning to expand by adding three new schools to its roster. Persistent rumors suggested that those three teams would be lured away from the Big East and that Miami would be one of them. The other two appeared to be Boston College and Syracuse, both of which had been in contact with ACC officials. The five other Big East football schools filed lawsuits to prevent the moves. In the end, the ACC invited Miami and Virginia Tech to join its conference, and both schools accepted the offer in June 2003.

Breaking Up Is Hard to Do

Losing its two most dominant football teams almost killed the Big East. Worried that the conference would lose its BCS bid, Big East executives considered abandoning football or breaking up the conference altogether. They finally decided to keep the conference together by replacing Miami and Virginia Tech with other schools. By October, the University of Louisville and the University of Cincinnati had agreed to join the Big East to bring the number of football teams back up to eight. But the upheaval was not over yet. Later that month, Boston College announced that it was leaving the Big East to join the ACC. Working fast, Tranghese found a replacement in the University of South Florida. Yet these new teams did not officially begin playing as Big East teams until the 2005–2006 season.

The 2004–2005 football season was a strange one for the conference. Miami and Virginia Tech were gone, but Boston College didn't complete its move to the ACC in time for the beginning of the football season, so it was still stuck in the conference for another year. The University of Connecticut, which had long been a dominant basketball power for the Big East, improved its football program enough to join Division I-A and become the Big East's seventh football team.

Meanwhile, Temple was struggling to attract fans to its football games. In 2004, the team failed to meet the Big East's minimum ticket sales requirements and had to drop out of the conference following the end of the season.

TV coverage of Big East games has helped the conference to attract fans. This camera is recording a Rutgers game in 2005.

A New Look for the Big East

On July 1, 2005, the Big East finally completed its reconstruction when Louisville, Cincinnati, and South Florida officially joined the conference, along with two other basketball-only schools. The conference was back to sixteen teams for basketball and eight for football. However, the Big East's new teams all came from Conference USA (a fifteen-member conference of Southern and Midwestern schools), which suddenly found itself with a shortage of teams. This

CURRENT BIG EAST TEAMS AND THEIR ACCOMPLISHMENTS

SCHOOL	TEAM NAME	YEAR JOINED BIG EAST	CONFERENCE CHAMPIONSHIPS	# OF BOWL APPEARANCES	BOWL W-L RECORD
University of Cincinnati	Bearcats	2005	0	9	5–4
University of Connecticut	Huskies	2004	0	1	1–0
University of Louisville	Cardinals	2005	1	13	6–6–1
University of Pittsburgh	Panthers	1991	1	24	10–14
Rutgers University	Scarlet Knights	1991	0	3	1–2
University of South Florida	Bulls	2005	0	2	1–1
Syracuse University	Orange	1991	4	22	12–9–1
West Virginia University	Mountaineers	1991	4	26	11–15

led to a chain reaction of conference realignments that changed the membership of five other college sports conferences as well.

This shifting of teams and scramble for replacements prompted by the Big East's reconstruction didn't win the conference any friends. Other conferences complained that the Big East should lose its automatic BCS bid because of its diminished status as a football power. Fans and the sports media criticized the Big East football program for trailing far behind the conference's basketball program in quality and popularity.

More and better television coverage and smarter scheduling have helped, but what has truly saved Big East football is the success of its teams. Since the 2005 realignment, Rutgers, Louisville, and West Virginia have proven themselves against some of the country's best teams. Big East football may not have the impressive

MOST RECENT BOWL APPEARANCE	# OF PLAYERS TO WIN HEISMAN	1ST-ROUND NFL DRAFT PICKS	# OF PLAYERS IN NFL HALL OF FAME	# OF PLAYERS/ COACHES IN NCAA HALL OF FAME
2007 International Bowl: Cincinnati 27, Western Michigan 24	0	0	0	3
2004 Motor City Bowl: Connecticut 39, Toledo 10	0	0	0	0
2006 Orange Bowl: Louisville 24, Wake Forest 13	0	3	1	0
2005 Fiesta Bowl: Utah 35, Pittsburgh 7	1	14	4	22
2006 Texas Bowl: Rutgers 37, Kansas State 10	0	0	0	5
2006 Papajohns.com Bowl: South Florida 24, East Carolina 7	0	0	0	0
2004 Champ Sports Bowl: Georgia Tech 51, Syracuse 14	1	9	5	12
2007 Gator Bowl: West Virginia 38, Georgia Tech 35	0	4	2	8

history of the Big Ten or the Southeastern Conference (SEC), but it has earned the respect of fans and other teams and conferences. "This league is where it is today because of Mike Tranghese," Louisville athletic director Tom Jurich said in a 2006 interview with the *New York Times*. "He had a ship with a bunch of cracks in it and not only patched them, but rebuilt it to the envy of a lot of people."

Against all odds, the Big East is not only still alive, it is also one of the most promising college football conferences in the country.

2 CHAPTER

Legendary and Winning Coaches

Given how young the Big East is and how modest its football program has been until recently, it may be hard to believe that one of the greatest college football coaches of all time coached at Big East schools.

"Pop" Warner

The Big East's coaching superstar can be found at the University of Pittsburgh—or at least he could have been found there from 1915 through 1923.

Glenn "Pop" Warner was a coaching genius almost from day one. Hired to coach the University of Georgia team in 1895, Warner had no athletic facilities and only thirteen players, but he still managed to squeeze out three wins in seven games. In Warner's second year, the team went undefeated. Success followed Warner everywhere he

Coach Glenn "Pop" Warner brought big changes not just to Pitt football, but also to the way that the game is played. Many of his innovations are still in practice today—such as the screen pass—as is the youth football league he founded.

took his coaching career: first Georgia and then Iowa State, Cornell, Carlisle Indian Industrial School, back to Cornell, and then back again to Carlisle. Warner had a bit of help at Carlisle from a player named Jim Thorpe, who became one of America's most famous and talented athletes of all time.

In 1914, Warner finally made his way to Pittsburgh. He coached the Panthers to thirty-three straight wins and two national championships. In his nine years at Pittsburgh, the Panthers had a record of sixty wins and only twelve losses, with four ties. So, what was it that made Warner so successful? Innovation. Football was still a relatively new sport when Warner began his coaching career, and he made it grow up in a hurry. He introduced many new plays and ideas that we now take for granted. The screen pass, the three-point stance, single- and double-wing formations, and the spiral punt are all Warner inventions. So are more fundamental things like putting numbers on players' jerseys and having them wear shoulder pads.

When "Pop" Warner retired in 1938, he was the winningest college coach in the game. But despite all of his victories and innovations, many Americans primarily remember him for starting the Pop Warner Little Scholars youth football league, which still exists today.

Syracuse's Award Winners

Plenty of other Big East schools have had prominent coaches. Syracuse, for example, boasts two National Coach of the Year Award winners in Ben Schwartzwalder and Dick MacPherson.

Schwartzwalder guided the team to its first bowl appearance in 1953, followed by another in 1957 and still another in 1959.

The 1959 season was a magical one for Syracuse—the team went undefeated and won the national championship, and Schwartzwalder was voted National Coach of the Year. He is also in the College Football Hall of Fame.

After a rough patch in the 1970s, Dick MacPherson took the helm in 1981. He earned his Coach of the Year Award in 1987 by coaching the team to an 11-0 record in the regular season. Over the next fourteen seasons, MacPherson and his replacement, Paul Pasqualoni, took Syracuse to eleven bowl games and four Big East championships.

Cincinnati's Sid Gillman

Cincinnati has four head coaches enshrined in the College Football Hall of Fame. One of them, Sid Gillman, is one of the few college

Pitt Coaching Factory

It's common for successful college coaches to move on to the NFL. But the University of Pittsburgh is unique in its high number of players who have ended up coaching in the pros. The most well known is probably Mike Ditka, whose fantastic playing career was almost matched by his success as a coach. Ditka coached the Chicago Bears for eleven years, including their victory in Super Bowl XX in 1986. But Ditka is not the only former Panther to coach a Super Bowl winner. Jimmy Johnson's five years as head coach of the Dallas Cowboys included consecutive Super Bowl victories in 1992 and 1993. Marty Schottenheimer has not won a Super Bowl like some of his fellow Panthers. In fact, he holds the record as the winningest modern coach who has never coached a team in the Super Bowl. His long career includes head coaching jobs with the Cleveland Browns, Kansas City Chiefs, Washington Redskins, and San Diego Chargers.

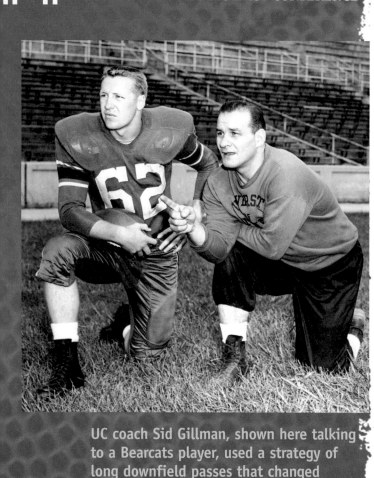

UC coach Sid Gillman, shown here talking to a Bearcats player, used a strategy of long downfield passes that changed football forever.

coaches also enshrined in the Pro Football Hall of Fame. Gillman developed a passing attack that the Bearcats continued to use for years after he left. His 50–13–1 record in six seasons as head coach in the 1940s and 1950s is the best of any UC coach. Those six years included three conference titles and two bowl game appearances.

West Virginia's Don Nehlen

Any conversation about great WVU coaches begins and ends with Don Nehlen. In twenty-one years at West Virginia, Nehlen did a lot more than win 149 games and take the team to eight major bowls. He also introduced the team's first home and away uniforms and the "Flying WV" logo that has since been adopted by the entire West Virginia athletic department.

Nehlen's Mountaineers went undefeated in 1988 before losing to Notre Dame in the Fiesta Bowl. They went undefeated yet again in 1993, winning the Big East conference championship. His final act as WVU coach was to lead the team to victory in the 2000 Music City Bowl. He was inducted into the College Football Hall of Fame in 2005.

Don Nehlen didn't just improve the way the Mountaineers played football;
he also improved the way they looked. Here, Nehlen is standing with guard
Jim LeBlanc during a 1993 victory. LeBlanc's helmet is decorated with the
"Flying WV" logo that Nehlen introduced.

The Rutgers Renaissance

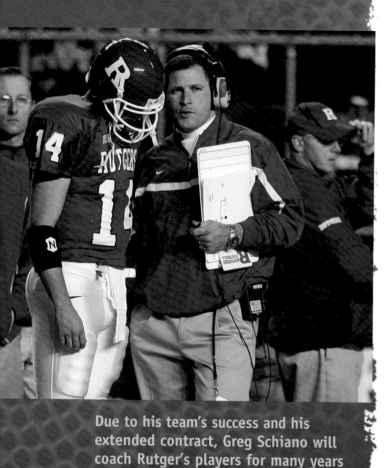

Due to his team's success and his extended contract, Greg Schiano will coach Rutger's players for many years to come.

George "Sandy" Sanford and Harvey Harman led Rutgers to early success in the first half of the twentieth century. But the best coach Rutgers has ever had might very well be their current coach, Greg Schiano. In 2006, Schiano led the team to its best season in thirty years and into the national spotlight. The Scarlet Knights finished the season ranked twelfth in the country, their highest ranking since 1961. Schiano won three different Coach of the Year awards and a contract extension that will keep him at Rutgers through the 2016 season.

3 CHAPTER

Notable Games and Important Firsts

The Big East hasn't been around as long as some of the more historic college football conferences, but it still has seen its share of memorable games. In fact, some of the most thrilling games in the Big East's short history came in just the past few years. But the 2006 Sugar Bowl might very well be the single most important game in the history of the conference.

No Respect

In 2005, the rebuilt Big East had just completed its first season with its new roster of teams. In the year and a half since Miami had left the conference, the Big East had been listening to constant criticism of its football program. Pittsburgh's big loss in the 2004 Fiesta Bowl only had made things worse. Critics were calling for the conference to lose its automatic bowl bid. So, when West Virginia

Georgia's Tony Milton (9) and Bryan McClendon (16) tackle West Virginia punter Phil Brady, but not before he turned a fake punt into a first down that iced WVU's Sugar Bowl victory in January 2006.

was invited to play in the Sugar Bowl after the 2005 season, the Mountaineers enjoyed little respect and were considered the underdog against hugely favored Georgia.

From the opening kickoff, West Virginia did its best to silence its critics and those of the Big East in general. The Mountaineers scored twenty-one points in the first quarter and another seven at the beginning of the second. Still, Georgia refused to go down easy. Late in the game, the Mountaineers were trying to hold onto a 38–35 lead when it looked like they were going to have to punt on fourth down. Georgia was going to get the ball back for one last chance to win the game. Instead, West Virginia coach Rich Rodriguez called a fake punt that caught Georgia by surprise and gained the Mountaineers a crucial first down. They kept the ball and the lead, and the win gave Big East football some much-needed respect.

Mountaineers Halt Rising Rutgers

Rutgers was unranked when the 2006 season began, but a 9–0 start got the team noticed. Suddenly, the national sports media was talking about Rutgers as a possible contender for the national championship. To get there, the Scarlet Knights first would have to get through Louisville, which also was undefeated and ranked third in the country. Rutgers beat Louisville to jump up to sixth in the BCS rankings, but then lost to Cincinnati to ruin its undefeated record. With Rutgers and Louisville each having lost only one game, the Big East championship and an invitation to a prestigious bowl game were up for grabs with one game left to play.

Needing a win, Rutgers faced West Virginia in the last game of the regular season. Rutgers played well, but the Mountaineers matched Rutgers every step of the way through all four quarters and two overtimes. West Virginia's starting quarterback Pat White went down with an injury. Amazingly, the team's backup quarterback saved the day for the Mountaineers. Jarrett Brown came off the bench to pass for 244 yards and ran for seventy-three more, including a touchdown. Despite Brown's heroics, the play of the day was a defensive one. West Virginia stopped a two-point conversion in the game's final seconds to preserve its lead and beat Rutgers.

Meanwhile, Louisville won its game and took the Big East title, but Rutgers's cinderella season was still its best in forty-five years and earned it an invitation to the Texas Bowl, where the Scarlet Knights beat Kansas State to further cement the Big East's new and

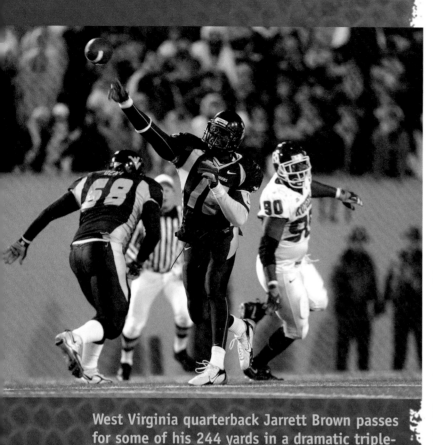

West Virginia quarterback Jarrett Brown passes for some of his 244 yards in a dramatic triple-overtime victory over Rutgers. The loss was one of only two for Rutgers in its 2006 season.

growing reputation as a football power to be reckoned with and respected.

Famous Firsts

Most Big East schools have been around for decades and played in many memorable games before joining the conference.

Cincinnati, which began playing football in 1885, has been involved in many firsts. For instance, it played to a scoreless tie in the state of Ohio's first intercollegiate football game against neighboring Miami University back in 1888, touching off one of the country's oldest intrastate college rivalries. Earlier that same year, the Cincinnati Bearcats played in what is believed to be college football's first postseason championship game when they were invited to New Orleans to play the Southern Athletic Club on New Year's Day. Cincinnati won the game and then responded to a challenge issued by Louisiana State University to play them the following day. Cincinnati won that game, too. In 1923, the team hosted the Midwest's first nighttime football game, which it won 17–0 over Kentucky Wesleyan University.

Miami University of Ohio was one of the first colleges to field a football team. But even this old photo, showing an MU team from the 1890s, was taken almost thirty years after Rutgers and the College of New Jersey (now Princeton) played in the first college football game.

The biggest first of them all, however, belongs to Rutgers, which played in the very first football game between two colleges. Rutgers and Princeton were the only two schools playing the new sport of football when they faced off on November 6, 1869. Rutgers won that game by a score of six runs to four. A week later, the two teams faced off again, and this time Princeton came out on top, 8–0. A planned third game between the schools was cancelled, so college football's first season ended with both teams holding a 1–1 record.

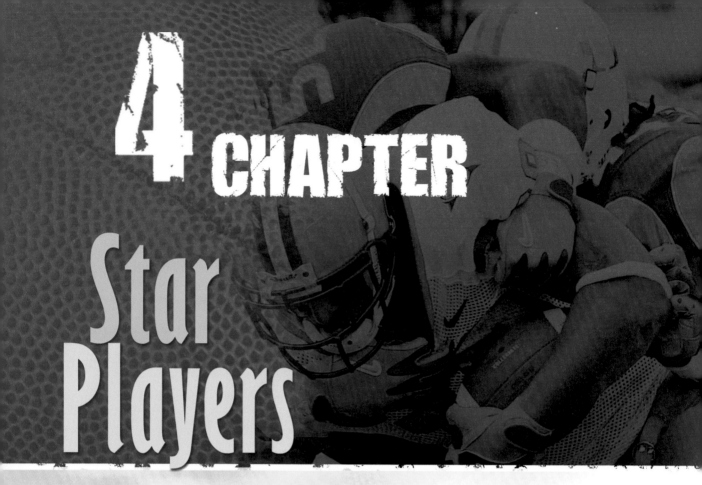

4 CHAPTER

Star Players

The Big East Conference has only recently started to regain its reputation as a top football conference, but Big East teams (past and present) have featured some of the greatest players the game has ever seen. From football legends like Johnny Unitas, Mike Ditka, Dan Marino, and Curtis Martin, to current NFL superstars like Donovan McNabb, Jeremy Shockey, Ray Lewis, and Michael Vick, Big East schools truly have been blessed.

University of Pittsburgh

Some of the most distinguished players in the NFL Hall of Fame wore the Pitt Panthers jersey. Dan Marino, Tony Dorsett, and Mike Ditka were all Panthers before they became legends.

Dan Marino is the most prolific passer in NFL history. He was the first player ever to pass for 5,000 yards in a season, and he

Panthers quarterback Dan Marino, shown here escaping a Penn State defender, went on to become one of the greatest quarterbacks in NFL history.

chalked up a total of thirteen 3,000-yard seasons. Over the course of his 242-game career with the Miami Dolphins, Marino completed 4,967 of 8,358 passes for 61,361 yards and threw 420 touchdowns. However, like other legends, Marino initially was underestimated by many NFL teams. During the 1983 draft, Marino was only the twenty-seventh overall pick. But once he took the field with the Miami Dolphins, there was no doubting his ability.

Tony Dorsett was a superstar running back at Pitt before he ever got to the NFL. Dorsett won the 1976 Heisman Trophy and was the Dallas Cowboys' number-one draft pick in 1977. From the outset, he was an offensive force to be reckoned with. In his rookie year in the NFL, he rushed for 1,007 yards and twelve touchdowns, winning Offensive Rookie of the Year honors. By the end of his career, Dorsett had 12,739 yards rushing, 398 receptions for 3,554 yards, and ninety-one touchdowns. He played in five NFC Championship games and two Super Bowls.

Mike Ditka was yet another Pitt Panther who met high expectations after college. Drafted as the Chicago Bears' number-one pick in 1961, Ditka was seen by many as the best tight end in the game. Not only did Ditka fit the traditional tight-end mold as a hard-hitting and sturdy blocker, but he was also a talented receiver. In his first season, he tore through defenses with fifty-six catches for 1,076 yards and twelve touchdowns, earning Rookie of the Year honors. Ditka overcame an injury-prone stint with the Philadelphia Eagles from 1967 to 1969 and moved to the Dallas Cowboys, where he won his first and only Super Bowl in 1971. He was the first tight end to be inducted into the Hall of Fame, but he also found great success as a coach, leading the Chicago Bears to a Super Bowl win in 1986.

Syracuse University

The Syracuse Orange have had a roller-coaster history when it comes to football. But the high points have been very high, thanks in large part to some of the best players the game has ever seen.

Jim Brown fits that description as well as anyone. At Syracuse, he excelled in basketball and lacrosse in addition to leading the football team to the 1957 Cotton Bowl. His skills as a versatile running back who could also catch passes and return kickoffs were no secret, and he was selected by the Cleveland Browns in the first round of the 1957 NFL draft.

Sometimes it seemed like nobody could stop Jim Brown *(top left)*. The running back was known for breaking tackle after tackle, first for Syracuse and later for the NFL's Cleveland Browns.

Brown started breaking records and winning awards almost immediately. He was Rookie of the Year in 1957 and MVP in 1957, 1958, 1963, and again in 1965. He led the league in rushing eight of the nine years he played, and he was elected to the Pro Bowl each of those nine years. He even threw three touchdown passes. Brown stunned the world by retiring when he was only thirty years old and still at the top of his game. Even though his career was shorter than those of many other leading pro football players, his career stats placed him far ahead of any player who had come before him and most who came after. As if there needs to be any further evidence of just how broad his incredible talent was, Brown is enshrined not just in the Pro Football Hall of Fame, but in the Lacrosse Hall of Fame as well.

Syracuse has had only one national title and one Heisman Trophy winner, and Ernie Davis was responsible for both. As a sophomore running back wearing Jim Brown's old number "44," Davis led the 1959 Syracuse team to an undefeated season. He was named MVP of the Cotton Bowl as the team won the national football championship. Two years later, Davis became the first African American to win the Heisman Trophy.

The Washington Redskins selected Davis as the first player taken in the 1962 NFL draft and then quickly traded his rights to the Cleveland Browns, where he would have played alongside fellow Syracuse alumnus Jim Brown. The two could have formed the most powerful running back duo of all time, but Davis was stricken with leukemia and died before ever playing a professional game. The Browns retired his number "45," even though he never played for them. In 2005, Syracuse retired uniform number "44," which had been worn by Davis, Brown, and other Orange greats.

Syracuse's impressive tradition of producing dominant running backs continued in the 1960s with standouts Floyd Little (who also wore number "44") and Hall of Famer Larry Csonka. A list of other notable Orangemen reads like a roll call of all-time greats: Hall of Famers John Mackey and Jim Ringo; standouts like Art Monk, all-time school rushing leader Joe Morris, and Heisman runner-up Don McPherson; and modern-day stars like quarterback Donovan McNabb and wide receiver Marvin Harrison. McNabb, in fact, was one of the most dominant college players in Big East history and still holds several conference and school records.

Big East Award Winners

The following list highlights some of the Big East players who have won national awards. While there are many honors awarded to college football players each year, the ones mentioned here are a few of the most prestigious. Many of these players have gone onto successful careers in professional football.

Heisman Trophy
(Nation's Best Player)

Year	Player	School
1961	Ernie Davis	Syracuse
1976	Tony Dorsett	Pittsburgh
1992	Gino Torretta	Miami

Butkus Award
(Nation's Best Linebacker)

Year	Player	School
2000	Dan Morgan	Miami

Bronko Nagurski Award
(Nation's Best Defensive Player)

Year	Player	School
1994	Warren Sapp	Miami
1999	Corey Moore	Virginia Tech
2000	Dan Morgan	Miami
2005	Elvis Dumervil	Louisville

Lombardi Trophy
(Nation's Best Lineman-Offensive or Defensive)

Year	Player	School
1980	Hugh Green	Pittsburgh
1994	Warren Sapp	Miami
1999	Corey Moore	Virginia Tech

Paul "Bear" Bryant Award
(Nation's Coach of the Year)

Year	Player	School
1959	Ben Schwartzwalder	Syracuse
1973	Johnny Majors	Pittsburgh
1976	Johnny Majors	Pittsburgh
1987	Dick MacPherson	Syracuse
1999	Frank Beamer	Virginia Tech
2001	Larry Coker	Miami

University of Cincinnati

While some teams name an award after one of their most inspiring players, the University of Cincinnati named its stadium after a departed football hero. During the last game of the 1923 season, Bearcat Jimmy Nippert was spiked in a game against state rival Miami University. Medical care was not nearly as advanced in those days, and Nippert soon contracted blood poisoning as a result of the wound. He died a month later. In memory of his grandson, Nippert's grandfather James Gamble donated the $250,000 that was needed to complete construction of the school's football stadium. Today, the Bearcats still play in James Gamble Nippert Memorial Stadium.

West Virginia University

The West Virginia University Mountaineers have had their fair share of stars at the line of scrimmage. In fact, the numbers speak for themselves: eleven All-Americans, 132 players drafted by the NFL, and two Pro Football Hall of Famers, including Sam Huff.

Sam Huff's is a truly unique story, filled with fateful discoveries and a rise to stardom. Huff was first discovered while still a junior in high school. A West Virginia coach had come to Huff's school to recruit one of his teammates, but the coach was so impressed by Huff that he ended up recruiting him instead. Huff went on to become an All-American offensive guard for the Mountaineers.

After an impressive college career, history repeated itself. New York Giants scout Al DeRogatis went down to West Virginia to take a look at another All-American guard named Bruce Bosley. But just like in high school, once the scout got a load of Huff, there was no turning back.

Huff started his pro career slowly when Giants coach Jim Lee Howell couldn't figure out where to play him. Then the starting middle linebacker Ray Beck got hurt, and the decision was made for Howell and Huff. Once Sam Huff stepped into that linebacker position, his career took off. He was named the Top NFL Linebacker in 1959 and went on to play in five Pro Bowls and six NFL title games. He even found himself on the cover of *Time* magazine and the subject of a TV special called "The Violent World of Sam Huff." Huff was inducted into the NFL Hall of Fame in 1982.

In addition to their two NFL Hall of Famers, West Virginia claims numerous other notable football alumni. On offense, there were

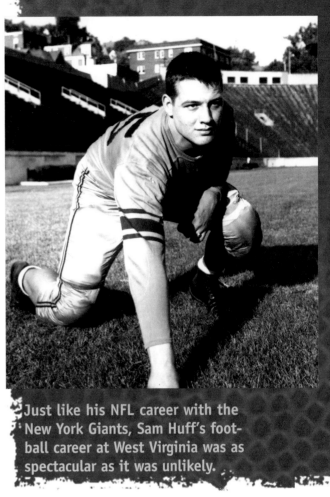

Just like his NFL career with the New York Giants, Sam Huff's football career at West Virginia was as spectacular as it was unlikely.

School Spirit Forever

School spirit can last long after graduation. Former Syracuse quarterback (and current Philadelphia Eagles star) Donovan McNabb is still closely involved with his alma mater: McNabb sits on Syracuse University's Board of Directors. You might say that former West Virginia quarterback Jeff Hostetler took school spirit to a whole new level. He spent a year as captain of the team, but much more impressive was when he married the daughter of his coach, Don Nehlen.

quarterbacks Major Harris and Jeff Hostetler (winner of Super Bowl XXV with the New York Giants), and on defense were linebackers Renaldo Turnbull and Darryl Talley.

University of Louisville

The only number ever retired by the Louisville Cardinals is the number "16" of Johnny Unitas, perhaps the greatest quarterback in the history of the game. A member of the class of 1955, Unitas was a lackluster ninth-round draft pick for the Pittsburgh Steelers. Unhappy with their choice, the Steelers committed what may be one of football's biggest blunders ever and cut Unitas before he got to throw a single pass in a game.

Determined to play, Unitas signed on to a semipro team for $6 a game until the Baltimore Colts picked him up the next season. Unitas was supposed to be only a backup, but got a chance to prove himself when an injury took the Colts' starter out in the fourth game of the season. Even though Johnny U's first pass was intercepted for a touchdown, he got over his rocky start to become a football legend.

Johnny U really became a household name after his performance in the 1958 NFL Championship game. Masterminding and executing a last-minute, eighty-yard drive in overtime to beat the Giants, Unitas's skill and poise were finally on display for a national television audience.

Unitas finished his career with 40,239 yards, 290 passing touchdowns, a record forty-seven straight games in which he passed for at least one touchdown, three years as NFL Player of the Year, and ten Pro Bowl appearances. To this day, every Louisville player makes a point of touching the statue of Johnny Unitas at the north end zone of Cardinal Stadium as he enters the field.

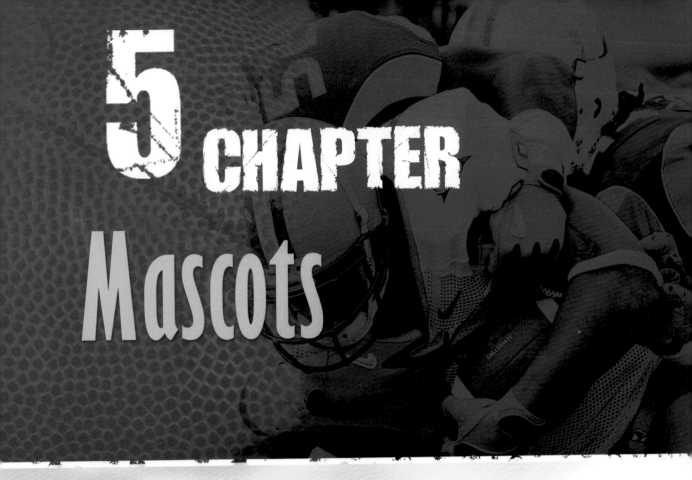

5 CHAPTER

Mascots

College sports have some of the country's most interesting mascots, and the Big East is no different. Wild animals, knights, mountain men, and even citrus fruits all do their best to inspire their home schools to victory.

Pet ROC

ROC the Panther has been leading the cheers at Pitt games for years. ROC, who is a costumed mascot, wears a Pitt jersey with the number "00" and entertains fans with acrobatics that include crowd surfing, break dancing, slam dunking at basketball games, and spiking footballs. It's no coincidence that ROC's fur color (officially called Vegas Gold) and eye color (navy) are also Pitt's school colors.

Named after beloved Panther Steve Petro, Pitt's mascot ROC is the Panther that now inspires the team's players and fans.

The name ROC is also quite intentional. The Pitt panther is named for Steve Petro, a former player, coach, and administrator at the school who was known as "the rock upon which Pitt football grew." School folklore says Petro so impressed coach Jock Sutherland in practices leading up to the 1937 Rose Bowl that Sutherland promoted him from third-string to starting guard for the game. The move paid off, and Pitt won the game 21–0. After graduation, Petro played pro football and then served in the army before coming back to Pitt as an assistant coach. After twenty-two years on the Pitt sidelines, he was appointed assistant to the athletic director, where he stayed until finally retiring in 1984. Two campus facilities, a scholarship fund, and the Pitt mascot are all named for Petro, the rock of Pitt football.

Pitt has had a panther as its mascot since 1909, when student George Baird first suggested the animal. Baird reasoned that panthers had once been native to the area and were similar in color to the gold that was one of the school's colors. His final

The Louisville Cardinal might not have the most original name, but you wouldn't want to get on his bad side.

reason was that no other university was using a panther as a mascot at the time.

Perhaps Louisville should have taken a lesson from Pitt and gone for originality. Instead, Louisville selected the cardinal as the symbol of its athletic teams because the cardinal is Kentucky's state bird. However, the cardinal is also the Missouri state bird, and Louisville shares its team name and mascot with countless other professional, college, and youth teams around the country. Today, the Louisville Cardinal appears as a red-and-black costumed mascot.

What's in a Name?

Pitt may have named its mascot after a former player, but that won't impress the folks at Cincinnati—they named their *team* after one of its players!

During a 1914 football game between Cincinnati and the University of Kentucky Wildcats, UC cheerleader Pat Lyon was impressed with UC fullback Leonard "Teddy" Baehr. "They may be Wildcats," Lyon chanted, "but we have a Baehr-cat on our side." The Cincinnati fans responded by cheering, "Come on, Baehr-cat!" A few days later, the UC student newspaper published a cartoon that showed the Kentucky Wildcat being chased by an animal labeled "Cincinnati Bear Cat," and the name stuck. By 1919, the media was calling the team Bearcats, and that's been its name ever since. An actual bearcat—a type of large cat from Malaysia—lives at the Cincinnati zoo and often attends UC home games.

The University of Connecticut also named its mascot after a real person. However, UConn's inspiration was a state politician, rather than a student. Because the school was called Connecticut Agricultural College originally, its athletic teams were initially known as the Aggies. In 1933, the school changed its name to Connecticut State College and its teams became the Statesmen. That didn't last long. In 1934, a Siberian husky named Jonathan, in honor of eighteenth-century Connecticut governor Jonathan Trumbull, made its first appearance on campus, and the husky was chosen as the school's mascot. A series of huskies, all white with one brown eye and one blue eye and all named Jonathan, have been used as mascots in the years since.

But aside from Jonathan and the costumed husky that also appears at UConn games, huskies are not native to Connecticut. So, why the husky? One often-stated theory is that it's a play on the UConn name, which sounds like Yukon, a territory in Canada where huskies actually can be found. Yet this doesn't solve the mystery because the husky was used as Connecticut's mascot long before the school started using the UConn nickname. In any case, Jonathan is here to stay. A statue of him sits near the entrance to the school's indoor swimming pool and often gets its nose rubbed by students looking for good luck.

The Syracuse . . . Orange?

Many schools choose ferocious animals, larger-than-life heroes, and warriors for mascots. Then there's Syracuse, whose students cheer for a smiling piece of fruit. Of course, Otto the Orange seems downright fierce compared to the school's previous mascot, the Saltine Warrior.

Actually, the Saltine Warrior was not a cracker but a Native American warrior named after both the plentiful salt deposits in the

A True Fighting Spirit

If you recognize the name Patrick Henry Hughes, it's probably because you've seen him on television or read about him in any of a number of newspapers or magazines around the world that have written about him and his father. Hughes is a trumpet player in the University of Louisville marching band, despite being blind and confined to a wheelchair. So, how does someone born with a disability that prevents him from walking join a marching band? His dedicated father, who is also named Patrick, stands behind Hughes and pushes his wheelchair through the band's routines. The elder Patrick has adjusted his work schedule so that he can be at every practice and every game, helping Patrick Henry fulfill his dream and inspire countless spectators with his talent and determination.

area surrounding the Syracuse campus and a campus archaeological dig that turned up artifacts from a Native American warrior. A costumed warrior began showing up at Syracuse football games in the 1950s, and the tradition continued until 1978, when school officials banned the Saltine Warrior to avoid offending Native Americans. A Roman warrior briefly took its place as mascot, but in 1982, an orange with arms, legs, and a cartoon face took over the job.

Sharing the school's official color, the orange stuck. Eight years later, he got an updated look and a new name: Otto. Still, it wasn't until 1995—thirteen years after he first appeared—that the university officially adopted Otto the Orange as its mascot. At the time, the Syracuse athletic teams were known as the Orangemen and Orangewomen.

In 2004, all team names were officially changed to Orange, which is shorter, more closely tied to the school color, and works just as well for men, women, and oranges.

Scarlet Knights and Mountaineers

Orange was initially the school color at Rutgers also. But Rutgers players wore scarlet handkerchiefs to better stand out from the Princeton team (whose school colors are orange and black) at their historic first game in 1869. Soon the color became officially associated with the school.

Meanwhile, the Rutgers athletic teams were known as the Queensmen, a reference to Queen's College, which was Rutgers's name when the school first opened. But in 1925, the mascot was changed to a rooster named Chanticleer, a figure from a medieval fable who attempts to avoid and outwit a crafty fox. You can probably guess that the rooster mascot caused other schools to mock Rutgers for being "chicken." As a result, in 1955, Rutgers students held an election to pick a replacement. The Scarlet Knight was chosen, taking the school back to its royal roots.

One mascot that will never be accused of being soft is the Mountaineer. West Virginia's mascot made his debut in 1904, but didn't start appearing at WVU games until the 1920s. Each year a student group selects a new student to dress up in a custom-tailored buckskin costume to portray the mountaineer at WVU games. The costume includes a coonskin cap and a fully functioning flintlock rifle that is more than four feet long. Male students who are chosen typically grow a beard to go along with the costume, but the

Who's "chicken"? It took eighty-six years for Rutgers to pick the Scarlet Knight as its mascot after earlier choosing a rooster.

mountaineer sometimes has been female as well. Whoever wears the costume shoots the rifle, loaded with live gunpowder, after West Virginia touchdowns.

GLOSSARY

alignment The proper adjustment or organization of the parts of something.

alumnus A graduate or former student of a specific school.

commissioner A person chosen to lead an athletic association or league made up of teams or other types of affiliated organizations.

consecutive Following in order, one after another, without interruption.

credibility The quality of being worthy of confidence or trust.

diminish To make smaller or reduce.

enshrine To place something within a site of honor in order to memorialize a person, group, place, or event; star college football players are "enshrined" in the College Football Hall of Fame.

Heisman Trophy An award given once every year to the best college football player in America.

helm The location or post of central control from which activities are directed.

innovation The act of introducing something new, improved, or merely different.

lackluster Dull; ordinary; without brilliance.

prolific Producing something in large amounts and/or very often.

reconstruction The act of rebuilding something or making something over.

recruiting Attracting or enrolling new members.

underdog A person or team that is expected to lose in a contest or competition.

upset To defeat an opponent who is considered better or stronger and is favored to win.

American Football Coaches Association
100 Legends Lane
Waco, TX 76706
(254) 754-9900
Web site: http://www.afca.com

Big East Conference
222 Richmond Street, Suite 110
Providence, RI 02903
(401) 453-0660
Web site: http://www.bigeast.org

College Football Hall of Fame
111 South St. Joseph Street
South Bend, IN 46601
(800) 440-FAME (3263)
(574) 235-9999
Web site: http://www.collegefootball.org

National Association of Intercollegiate Athletics
23500 West 105th Street
Olathe, KS 66061
(913) 791-0044
Web site: http://naia.cstv.com/index.html

National Collegiate Athletic Association (NCAA)
700 W. Washington Street
P.O. Box 6222

Indianapolis, IN 46206-6222

(317) 917-6222

Web site: http://www.ncaa.org/wps/portal

National Football Foundation

22 Maple Avenue

Morristown, NJ 07960

(973) 829-1933

Web site: http://www.footballfoundation.com

National Junior College Athletic Association

1755 Telstar Drive, Suite 103

Colorado Springs, CO 80920

(719) 590-9788

Web site: http://www.njcaa.org/index.cfm

Pro Football Hall of Fame

2121 George Halas Drive NW

Canton, OH 44708

(330) 456-8207

Web site: http://www.profootballhof.com

Web Sites

Due to the changing nature of Internet links, Rosen Publishing has developed an online list of Web sites related to the subject of this book. This site is updated regularly. Please use this link to access the list:

http://www.rosenlinks.com/icf/fbec

FOR FURTHER READING

Curtis, Brian. *Every Week a Season: A Journey Inside Big-Time College Football*. New York, NY: Ballantine Books, 2004.

DeCock, Luke. *Great Teams in College Football History*. Chicago, IL: Raintree, 2006.

MacCambridge, Michael. *ESPN College Football Encyclopedia: The Complete History of the Game*. New York, NY: ESPN Books, 2005.

Mattern, Joanne. *Donovan McNabb: The Story of a Football Player*. Hockessin, DE: Mitchell Lane Publishers, 2004.

Ours, Robert M. *Bowl Games: College Football's Greatest Tradition*. Yardley, PA: Westholme Publishing, 2004.

Ours, Robert M. *College Football Encyclopedia: The Authoritative Guide to 124 Years of College Football*. Rocklin, CA: Prima Publishing, 1994.

Quirk, James. *The Ultimate Guide to College Football: Rankings, Records, and Scores of the Major Teams and Conferences*. Champaign, IL: University of Illinois Press, 2004.

Rockwell, Bart. *World's Strangest Football Stories*. Jefferson City, MO: Troll Communications, 2001.

BIBLIOGRAPHY

Boyles, Bob, and Paul Guido. *Fifty Years of College Football*. Phoenix, AZ: Sideline Communications, 2005.

Bradley, Michael. *Big Games: College Football's Greatest Rivalries*. Dulles, VA: Potomac Books, 2006.

MacCambridge, Michael. *ESPN College Football Encyclopedia: The Complete History of the Game*. New York, NY: ESPN Books, 2005.

Ours, Robert M. *Bowl Games: College Football's Greatest Tradition*. Yardley, PA: Westholme Publishing, 2004.

"Patrick Henry Hughes." PatrickHenryHughes.com. Retrieved March 2007 (http://www.patrickhenryhughes.com).

Quirk, James. *The Ultimate Guide to College Football: Rankings, Records, and Scores of the Major Teams and Conferences*. Champaign, IL: University of Illinois Press, 2004.

"ROC." PittsburghPanthers.com. 2007. Retrieved January 2007 (http://pittsburghpanthers.cstv.com/jrpanthers/rocsworld.html).

Smith, Ronald A. *Sports and Freedom: The Rise of Big-Time College Athletics*. New York, NY: Oxford University Press, 2001.

Thamel, Pete. "Rebuilt Big East Gets Big Bounce from Football." *New York Times*, Section D, p. 1, November 2, 2006.

Thelin, John R. *Games Colleges Play: Scandal and Reform in Intercollegiate Athletics*. Baltimore, MD: Johns Hopkins University Press, 1996.

Watterson, John Sayle. *College Football: History, Spectacle, Controversy*. Baltimore, MD: Johns Hopkins University Press, 2002.

Yarbrough, Roy E. *Mascots: The History of Senior College & University Mascots/Nicknames*. 2nd ed. California, PA: Bluff University Communication, 2005.

INDEX

About the Author

Adam B. Hofstetter is a weekly columnist for SportsIllustrated.com. He has written several sports books for Rosen Publishing, including a book about the Pacific-10 football conference. When he's not attending various sports events, Hofstetter can be found in New York, where he lives with his wife and their two children.

Photo Credits

Cover top, bottom, pp. 11, 19, 20, 24, 27 © Getty Images; pp. 1, 3 © www.istockphotos.com/Lewis Wright; pp. 4–5, 37 University of Louisville; pp. 5 top, 8, 9, 22 © AP Images; pp. 7, 41 Rutgers Athletics; pp. 12–13 © www.istockphotos.com/Jacom Stephens; pp. 15, 36 University of Pittsburgh; p. 18 University of Cincinnati; p. 25 Miami University Archives; p. 29 © Collegiate Images/Getty Images; p. 33 Collegiate Images.

Designer: Tom Forget
Photo Researcher: Marty Levick